How to Look Your Very Best Everyday

By

Krystal Flott

Copyright © 2022 by Krystal Flott

Print ISBN: 978-1-952561-19-1

All rights reserved. No part of this book may be reproduced in any form or by any electronic or mechanical means, including information storage and retrieval systems, without written permission from the author, except for the use of brief quotations in a book review.

Printed in the United States of America.

This book is dedicated to my mom and sister for their continious support.

CONTENTS

Introduction 1
Fashion Myths 3
How To Look Your Very Best Every Day 10
What To Wear For Different Occasions 12

Introduction

Every morning when you wake up, say "it is so fun getting dressed, I love my style, and I love my wardrobe", while looking in your mirror at your gorgeous self!!

Trends change so fast, styles and colors come and go. It's not always easy keeping up with TV shows, social media blogs, magazines, and the 'what's hot now' news. So, I have created this book to keep you in the know at all times. In this book, you will learn,

- How to rid yourself of old fashion beliefs
- How to dress for your body type
- How to keep up with new trends and not purchase new clothing
- How to transition your style with seasons and not purchase new clothing
- What colors work best for you
- What to wear for different occasions.

How to Look Your Very Best Everyday

With so many decisions we have to make in a day, looking our best shouldn't be one. Getting dressed should be fun and energizing because you know that you're about to turn heads effortlessly and feel good while doing so. How you look plays a very important role in your life, how you look determines how you feel, and how you feel determines your daily actions and achievements. So, let's look good, feel great and get things done!

Before we start with the good how to's, let's kill some old fashion lies that's been around for ages. You know the things our parents and grandparents have said like, it's written in stone, and you can't wear white after Labor Day, Myth!

Fashion Myths

> **Certain clothes only look good if your tall and skinny.**
> **Myth!**

The only reason why you believe this myth is because someone you trust said it. You can wear anything you want even if you go as far as tailoring your clothing to fit your body type. Do you really think all the tall and skinny people's clothing come to fit their body? NO! They have a seamstress, find yourself a great seamstress, and become their friend.

> **You can't wear gold and silver together.**
> **Myth!**

Blah blah blah! Myth! Think about your Christmas decorations, gold, and silver right? Think about New Year's Eve, or how about the various accessory companies that are now mixing two-tone necklace and bracelets together. I believe in standing out and doing what works best for you. Your attire and accessories should give you such confidence that you don't even hear what others think about mixing silver and gold. By the way, I love it and think it's so sexy.

> **You can't wear a monochrome look because it doesn't match. Myth!**

Says who? It matches perfectly! Look at how beautiful an eyeshadow palette is with the monochrome grey, pink, and blue. Oooh my God!! Art! An easy way to start wearing a monochrome look is to start with different shades of grey, example:

Top - soft/light grey

Bottom- dark grey/charcoal

Leggings (???) if needed- a soft black.

Shoe- suede grey (because one way is lighter than the other) let's be daring.

Horizontal stripes make you look heavy. Myth!

Nooooo!! Once again, since you heard someone say that now, you believe it, and it's true to you. Whatever size you are, that's what size you are. Be true to yourself about your appearance and your confidence; then you will see a drastic change in your wardrobe. Besides, wearing solids gets boring, so step out and wear those stripes tiger.

Never mix patterns, it looks too busy. Myth!

Tell the furniture store that when they mix the patterns in your carpet or your pillows on the couch or the chairs at your table. Patterns are so beautiful, and they complement one another. It's ok to wear flower and stripes or polka dots and plaid, but don't get out of hand.

How to Look Your Very Best Everyday

Sequins and sparkles are for evening wear only. Myth!

Oh, stop! Sequins and sparkles make me happy!! I'm sure if you were feeling down and saw someone bright and vibrant with a touch of style that would make you feel happy. It's nothing like dressing comfy with jeans and sneakers and a sequin tank, OH MY GOSH!! Can you say, style! Style! Style! Please! Loosen up; you can wear what you want when you want, there are no rules!

Never wear more than one bold color. Myth!

Oh! So, don't dress like the 90's is what you're saying? Why are two or three bold colors too much now and wasn't then? Think about that. It's all in how you wear it and where you wear it. A pop of bold color with a suit is always a go, a bold color top and shoe with a pattern pant or dress. Or maybe you're an office kind of person, put on your royal blue blazer and do business. Why not?! You have a new confidence now.

Your shoes, belt, and handbag have to match. Myth!

Why though? It's ok sometimes to follow this trend, but don't allow it to keep you in a box, even jack jumped out of the box. You can also color coordinate with your bag, shoes, and belt. Black shoe, pattern bag (multi colors), select a color from your bag that also matches your attire, can't forget about that, and be on your happy mixing colors way.

Never wear white after Labor Day. Myth!

This is when winter white comes out, and you mix it with your florals. And now, designers and retailers are stocking stores with white shoes right after Labor Day. Surprise! No one follows that trend anymore.

How to Look Your Very Best Everyday

> **Navy and black is to close to wear together. Myth!**

Navy and black actually complement each other, and it's very classic and classy. The look it gives is clean and modern. The two colors can be worn on the job as well after hours. You can't go wrong with the two, and yes, you can tell the difference between them.

> **Stockings and open toe shoes just don't look right together. Myth! Or you can say opinion.**

This is just an opinion of someone who thinks it's bazaar to wear leggings or stockings with open toe shoes. Of course, ladies on the runway do it all the time, but it's a pretty common, yet, outspoken look, you better have the right response for someone when they ask why. Well, because I like it and it looks good on me.

Krystal Flott

Nowadays, fashion is all about being bold and audacious. Forget about all those outdated myths and rules you were taught.

How To Look Your Very Best Every Day

When putting on your clothing for work, school, business, or date night, always ask yourself these questions:

1. Does this fit me properly? Is it too little or too big? You want your clothing to be just right, that's why it's always good to lay your clothing out in advance in case something happens like, "oh no! It's too little" now, what am I going to wear? Then, you just put on anything, stop it! Get yourself together in advance and make sure your clothes fit you properly.

2. Do these colors match or coordinate together? Make sure the color of your clothing match, and also, your clothing should match you and whatever day you are looking forward to. Are you going for a

business look today? Or are you going for a bold, vibrant, fashion look today? Whatever you choose to do, do it CONFIDENTLY for YOU!

3. Ask yourself what does this outfit say about me? Is it saying, I don't feel like being here? Is it saying, oh, I didn't prepare my clothing, excuse the wrinkles and stains? Or, is your outfit saying, hi everyone! I'm here! Confident and clean, ready for an awesome day? First impression is everything! It's very important, even if it's not your first day, people treat you how you look. Yes! It's true, the way you dress says a lot about you, try it and see.

What To Wear For Different Occasions

Always check out the place online that you're going to, look for, how's the atmosphere, how are the people dressed that go to this place, and so on. Remember, it's always better to be overdressed than underdressed.

Casual occasions; Networking, Business lunch, Office Party, Date, Church, or Dinner.

Ladies: Wear a pencil skirt or dress pants, paired with a blouse or button-down shirt and a pair of heels or wedges. You can also wear a dress, solid or pattern with a nice heel.

Gentlemen: Wear trousers with a polo collar shirt or button-down shirt, paired with a suede or leather driver. Men, you can also, wear a nice pair of denim with a button down shirt and blazer or sports coat, paired with a leather loafer or boot.

Krystal Flott

Business Casual Occasions: Business meeting, Daily work attire (office/corporate), or company party.

Ladies: wear a suit (black, blue, or grey), pants and jacket or skirt and jacket, with a blouse or button-down shirt with a pair of heels. Remember; always wear a shirt that is acceptable to wear without a jacket.

Gentlemen: wear a suit (black, blue, or grey), with a nice quality crew neck /V-neck shirt or button-down shirt, paired with leather loafers. Or men can wear dress pants with a button-down shirt and sweater vest, or vest with a boot or loafer.

Black Tie: Charity fundraiser, formal events, galas, auctions, weddings, some red carpet events, and night opera.

Now that it's 2022, everyone is fashion-forward, and there are no rules for most black tie events. You have those who are traditional and those who are fashion forward with their attire, and that's ok; it's enough creativity for us all.

How to Look Your Very Best Everyday

Ladies: we have so many options, floor-length ball gown or a fancy cocktail dress (short), depending on the venue. Also, ladies have separate kinds of wears to wear for these types of occasions; a short sleeve sequins top with a long satin skirt dusting the floor, and of course, long white gloves and pearls. Accessories are a must for ladies, a simple clutch to hold in your hand, a nice head piece of kneaded, elegant necklace with bold earrings or vice versa.

Men: Men, it's always ok to keep it simple, wearing a dark suit or tuxedo without tails, paired with a white shirt and tie. Some may prefer to wear a vest, and that's ok as well. You may also want to incorporate prints with your tie, or your socks or your shoes, come on guys! Let's jump out of the box and get trendy. Yes!! You are still a real man rocking prints. During the warm weather months, black tie events are the best for men. Wearing a nice crisp white dinner jacket in linen, gabardine, worsted wool, or cotton fabric material. Oh my Gosh!! Paired with a nice fragrance (Tom Ford, Creed, Bond No. 9, etc.) you have stolen the night my friend.

Going back to the beginning when we talked about morning affirmations, I love my wardrobe, well; you want to love how you look in your wardrobe as well. And knowing your body type is a great place to start. So, we created this section to help you discover your body type, and how to show off your favorite features, yes, you do have a favorite feature on your body. Well, if you don't, you will by the end of this section.

Pay attention to your curves. Look at how they connect your bust (chest), waist, and hips. If you have to measure yourself, get an accurate number for your bust, waist, and hips, even if you have to go to a cleaners or lingerie department store. Depending on the size of each part (inches) you will know exactly what your body type is, you are rather apple-shaped, pear-shaped, straight shaped, hourglass-shaped, or athletic shaped.

How to Look Your Very Best Everyday

Apple shape:

- Heavy top
- Well-proportioned
- Shoulders are broader than your hips
- Not as curvy around your hips (no definition in the waist)
- Wrap dress

With this body type, you should consider wearing, tops that compliment your chest, like, v- necks, plunging necklines, strapless, and scoop neck. This will take the attention away from the waist to the neckline. Also, consider wearing boot cut or wide leg pants with a heeled shoe to give an appearance of definition in the waistline and length in the torso.

To dress successfully for the apple body, wear clothing that accentuates other parts of your body besides the midriff.

Pear shape:

- Bottom heavy

- Narrow shoulders in comparison to your hips
- Opposite of apple shape
- Straight leg or skinny pants paired with a mid-length blazer to balance the round look for casual attire (Stepping out of the rules.)
- Wide leg pants with a fitted top for business attire paired with a heel
- Belted waist dress

With this body type, you should consider wearing, the perfect measured bra to enhance the chest and make your tops look slimmer and waistline in, hips out. For your bottom, wide leg or flare pants to balance the top and the bottom, paired with a heel.

To dress successfully for the pear body, wear clothing that accentuates other parts of your body besides your hips and butt.

Straight/ rectangular shape:

- No hips

How to Look Your Very Best Everyday

- Shoulders and waistline are the same measurements
- Choose a blazer or jacket with emphasis on the waist
- A good bra to lift the chest

With this body type, you may lack curves, but that's ok! We have so many accessories to add to your wardrobe like a belt, a ruffle blouse instead of plain, and tops or dresses with embellishments or just add jewelry.

To dress successfully for the straight body type, always add a layer like a blazer that has a tailored look in the waist and back. Add a belt around your waist with your tops or wear peplum like tops. And wear pants that define your waist and flare just a little in the legs.

Hourglass shape:

- Curvy
- Well defined waist

- Bust and hip measurements are fairly even
- Fuller bust, hips, and thighs

With this body type, you should consider wearing; tailored clothing usually fits better, seamstress knows how to balance your top and your bottom while accentuating your waist. V-neck tops are great but try to avoid tops that reveal too much cleavage, and run from tights to wear as clothing; I suggest only wearing them for exercise purposes only.

To dress successfully for the hourglass body, avoid any and everything that makes you look boxy, embrace your curves and conquer the world.

Athletic shape:

- Not curvy and not straight
- You are Muscular and toned
- Large bone structure
- Very nice definition in the arms and legs.
- Wear tops that define your waist like peplum shirts.

How to Look Your Very Best Everyday

- Wear a belt around your waist with dresses and jackets (trendy for a blazer and out of the box)
- Mid rise denim

With this body type, you should consider wearing, (you have so many options) quarter length sleeves make your arms appear not as muscular, or you may love your nice arms and go sleeveless (I would if I had nice arms), or you can get a sleeve that stops above the biceps.

To dress successfully for the athletic body, avoid any and everything that makes you look straight up and down. Embrace everything about you, muscles and all.

In conclusion, how to look your very best every day, one, I would say confidence in yourself, two, confidence in your body type, three, confidence in your wardrobe knowing what works for you, and four, knowing how to dress for success or that first impression. Remind yourself daily that this is not hard and you're not going to make this hard, because you are going to PREPARE! PREPARE! PREPARE! As the author and life coach Brian Tracy has said, "proper prior planning prevents poor performance".

Consider your options and always be open for change when shopping and getting dressed, and remember to throw away all those crazy myths about the do's and don't in fashion. Book yourself a professional bra fitting soon; it's going to change your life.

I hope you enjoyed this book as much as I did, I know you are ready to try some new things and switch up your old things. I send with you peace, love, and confidence. Thanks for reading.

See you soon,
Krystal Flott

www.ingramcontent.com/pod-product-compliance
Lightning Source LLC
Chambersburg PA
CBHW052130110526
44592CB00013B/1827